Side by Side: Golf Lessons with the Pro

Mahrty Lehr

With Laura Lewis

Published by BookLocker.com, Inc., St. Petersburg, Florida.

Printed on acid-free paper.

Booklocker.com, Inc.
2017

First Edition

Table of Contents

The Fundamentals

Chapter 1:
Meet Your New Golf Coach

Is your golf game plateaued? You can't figure out how to get to the next level? Do you keep repeating the same mistakes but don't know how to fix them? Perhaps you don't know what those mistakes are? Is your game inconsistent and unpredictable? You don't know why sometimes you do well and other times you don't?

You may think "well, that's golf."

Not true.

You *can* take your game to the next level, gain consistency, and I can help you. Teaching and helping people improve their game and their enjoyment of it is what I do best. I've spent a lifetime helping golfers to achieve their "aha" moments and to experience the immense satisfaction of a round well-played.

My name is Mahrty Lehr and you've probably not heard of me. That's all right. I will tell you a little bit about myself, and we can get to know each other. I have played golf since the age of six. I was offered a college scholarship in golf, but to be honest, being a student was never my thing. I joined the apprentice program of the PGA in 1967 and played the tour in 1973 and 1974.

Starting in 1967, I apprenticed under golf's premier instructor, Bob Toski, co-founder of the Golf Digest Instruction School, in Key Largo, Florida. Since that time I have provided professional golf instruction at golf and country clubs in Florida, Ohio, and Virginia and have been a PGA Class "A" professional for over 40 years.

This book is about and for you, the student; it is not about me. My passion and gift has always been in helping others dramatically improve their game, which is why I am so excited that you have picked up this book. We are going to do great things together!

Because you and I have likely not met yet, I will share a few kind words and testimonials from clients so you know you will be in good hands:

"I have been a PGA Professional since 1973. I have been to many teaching seminars, coaching clinics, and I worked with some of the best instructors in the country. I worked with Mahrty recently and he made more sense to me in 30 minutes than I have heard in 30 years. Mahrty has a unique ability to diagnose a problem, explain it in its simplest form, and help his pupils understand how to fix it." – Bobby Green, PGA

"Mahrty has the innate ability to take a look at your swing and immediately assess your particular issues. During one of my first swings he witnessed, he calmly said "I'll bet you are exhausted after your round of golf!" This was true – my hands hurt, my back ached, and I was always stiff after play – plus I didn't play well. He got me to relax my swing and loosen up – and really got me to enjoy the game again. Several times I have been on the range with Mahrty while other instructors were giving lessons. The biggest difference is that Mahrty gets you to visualize what he is telling you in ways you won't forget.

The best thing he has done for me is to help me understand when I don't hit a good shot, what I need to do to correct my swing, and get back on track when he isn't standing next to me. I now have the ability to understand my individual mechanics coupled with a mental checklist of what to do to make corrections when he isn't looking over my shoulder." – Doug Dorsey

"Mahrty Lehr is an old soul golf teacher. He patiently taught me the fundamentals of my golf swing in my 30's and 40's. Over the past 30 years of exploring, learning, and working on my swing technique, I am back to his original teachings. He is a diamond in the rough and knows the golf swing and really cares about his students. Mahrty Lehr has the pure wisdom and knowledge to create the most efficient motion for the golf swing." – Natalie Easterly

"Over the years I have had the privilege of taking lessons from Mahrty. I visit the Richmond area, where he resides, from Ohio once if not twice a year to take a lesson from him. Mahrty knows the golf swing so well and is able to detect a problem and correct that problem within minutes. He helped me to become a good golfer that is aware of her swing and understands it. Mahrty has taken me from a 19 handicap to the current 14, hitting the ball with accuracy." – Gayle Klump

"Before I started to work with him, I would consider myself to have been an average golfer, but under his guidance for the past four years, he has lowered my handicap by seven strokes to single digit status. I have won the past three consecutive Ladies Championships at our club and I attribute my success to his direction of my game. My husband and son have had equal success under his leadership and both have won VSGA tournaments as a result of the physical and mental preparation which Mahrty has given them." – Jeanie Bliley

"Mahrty has a way of reinforcing what he's taught you before in prior lessons without making you feel badly about not remembering them all. For example, if he's seeing something in my backswing that he doesn't like, he might say 'you remember what we said about how you start your backswing?' Looking for me to respond with 'my left shoulder.' He poses questions that force me to fill in the blanks with information he's already provided me, but does so in a reinforcing manner focused on the positive.

I have had lessons from several PGA pros and can say without reservation that Mahrty's style and manner of teaching is by far the best that I have experienced." – Clif Denney, Golf Operations Manager, Independence Golf Club Richmond VA

"The crux of what makes Mahrty different, I have learned, is his eyes. The man can see the slightest flinch of a muscle, movement of a thumb, or slight heel plant imperfection, all at full swing speed. Video is superfluous with him. He has seen it already and is well on his way into correction mode before the tape would be rewound. Narrowly focused on the fundamentals of body and swing, he worked to find the communication, not always verbal, which would demonstrate to each muscle or tendon the feel or direction needed to build a swing. Laying the foundation, each small incremental adjustment builds on the last to interlock all the pieces of the human jigsaw. When I have backtracked, because of his technique, he knows exactly where the flaw has originated, and we can build from that point forward again instead of remaking the whole." – Tyler Franks

I mention these only because I want you to know that the investment of time that you are about to make will be well worth it.

Numerous people have shaped the game of golf over the years. Here I am holding a collage that a colleague gave me of the three people I believe most influenced the game of modern golf: Ben Hogan, Bob Toski, and Arnold Palmer:

I keep this in my study so I am always reminded of their very significant contributions.

First, Ben Hogan. He wrote "Five Lessons: the Modern Fundamentals of Golf," the most read golf tutorial book ever because he put his finger on how the swing works and how the muscles interact with the swing. This book proves that understanding the game of golf doesn't have to be complicated. The 6 chapters of this book take a mere 114 pages. He was also a great golfer and won 9 major championships.

Next, Bob Toski. He was my mentor during my time in Florida. Since leaving the tour at age 30, he has been a significant instructor, teaching thousands of students, and co-founding the Golf Digest School. He is a great communicator with any range of people and in my opinion, being able to communicate effectively is what teaching is all about. Bob was inducted into the PGA Hall of Fame in 2013, a recognition well deserved.

Last, Arnold Palmer. Palmer and television came on the scene at the same time; he was very charismatic and expressive and the crowds loved him. Palmer truly popularized the game, and at 85 years old, he still ranks third in off-course dollars earned.

But enough about my heroes and me! On to you and your game. I measure my success by the success of my students. The best way to learn golf is the right way. Master the fundamentals and you will never look back. This book is great for both beginners and for individuals who want to take their game to the next level. We will focus on very specific techniques and I promise you will be very happy with the results.

Chapter 2:
Before We Start

Even though I won't be standing right next to you, I want you to feel as if I am. I have helped countless students improve their game and can't wait to do the same for you. If you have any questions after reading this book, please contact me at my website www.lehrgolf.com and we will work out a plan to put you on the path to success.

In all of my lessons, I ask the student to write down what we have talked about. You should keep a golf journal and add to it every time you take a lesson or practice. Write down which technique you are working on, how it feels, any challenges or successes, what you did differently or the same, and what you experimented with.

I would encourage you to find an instructor who does not play during your playing lesson, unless asked to show how to hit a particular shot. Playing lessons are a great way to put your whole game together but instructors should be focused on watching you play, so they can provide the best possible feedback. A lesson is all about and for you. This is what you are paying for. It is your game. The purpose of a playing lesson is not for an instructor to have a chance to play or to impress you.

I don't encourage video lessons in which you watch yourself swing unless you are more advanced in your game. What you feel when you swing and what you see on video are two different things. I prefer to work with the student on what a correct motion *feels* like. A video will never show you this. It will never show you the correct grip pressure, a sense of distance, or all of the other sensory experiences we will talk about. A skilled instructor will provide feedback after reviewing the ball's flight because she or he understands cause and effect, not because the instructor has the benefit of a video camera and monitor.

Whenever possible, I explain the reasons why a certain motion works or does not work. I do this because when you understand the physiological reasons for a particular result, it is easier for you to visualize, to remember, and to execute.

If you have read other books about golf, you will find that I have a very direct and easily understood way of communicating, which my students really appreciate. I don't waste a lot of time on baloney and I don't hold back any secrets. This will make the learning process as quick as possible for you.

We will talk a lot about your eyes. Everything you touch or do in golf is related to your eyes and we will work on the training of your eyes. We will discuss topics like choosing a target beyond the flag, picking different targets at the practice tee, positioning your feet while looking at the target, and more. It is vitally important to pay attention to where your eyes are focused, as this affects your body's positioning and movement.

Your hands will also serve as your eyes. Your hands are the only part of your body that touches the club and through which you can communicate with the clubhead. We will work on developing your feel for where the clubhead is during the swing and timing the release through the hitting area. When your hands can sense the relationship between the clubhead and the release, your hands are your eyes.

In addition to focusing on your eyes and sense of sight, we will also focus on developing other senses like touch, timing, weight, and distance. Occasionally, I will ask you to practice with your eyes shut, with the ball on a tee. When you do this, your other senses will be heightened. You will gain awareness of your muscles and the feel of certain motions, and of the weight and motion of the club. When you isolate your senses like this, your body, muscles, and memory actually retain more information and you will learn faster. By closing your eyes and paying closer attention to the muscles and their movements, I've had students actually diagnose their own errors and correct them.

One final note, all instructions are written for a right-handed person. If you are left-handed you will simply need to make the adjustment.

Chapter 3:
The Mind's Eye and Your Subconscious

I'd like to discuss a concept called The Mind's Eye, which is an important component of my teaching philosophy. The Mind's Eye is an abstract but very real concept, defined by Merriam-Webster as "the mental faculty of conceiving imaginary or recollected scenes." In the case of golf, we are talking about imagining the swing before you take it.

I will ask that as you are standing behind the ball at the address position that you envision yourself at address, making the correct swing, and taking the shot. Envision the ball's path and its landing. Why is this important? Because by doing so, you pre-program the subconscious and your muscles to create the shot you imagined.

If you have already hit the shot in your Mind's Eye, you have seen the result. When you step up to take the swing, you are simply repeating what you have already seen. By giving your body a chance to visualize the set up and swing, it will be easy for you to achieve your goal. You have pre-programmed your body to accomplish what your Mind's Eye has seen.

You can also try choosing a golf pro or athlete whose height and weight are similar to yours, and whose swing you like. Picture their swing before you make yours, and you are harnessing the power of The Mind's Eye.

The Mind's Eye and the subconscious work hand in hand. While the Mind's Eye might be like a cinematic experience in your imagination, the subconscious is the part of your mind that actually affects behavior and movement. Day in and day out, our subconscious runs our lives, and likewise, it can in the game of golf. When you walk, for example, you usually do not think about directing your legs to walk or telling them how to do it, they just do it. The same can be said for picking up a cup of coffee or any mindless movement we make throughout the day.

In the game of golf, if one or more of your fundamentals are not correct, I believe that your subconscious will instinctively realize this and will attempt to compensate by making adjustments to your movement or positioning. These types of manipulations will slow your club head speed, reduce your swinging power and distance, and play havoc with your ball dispersion.

If you are misaligned, or your grip pressure isn't maintained throughout the swing, or your posture is incorrect, your subconscious will attempt to compensate for these errors. In my opinion, you cannot train your subconscious, by definition it works on its own.

But good news! If you have everything lined up correctly and your fundamentals are in place, your subconscious will realize this. You will then be able to swing freely towards your intended target with no encumbrances. Eliminate all obstacles by mastering the fundamentals and nothing will hold you back.

I firmly believe that learning to engage your Mind's Eye and learning to free your subconscious is going to become the next frontier of instruction in many fields, not just golf. But for our purposes, you are now on the leading edge of golf instruction. Let's get started!

Chapter 4:
Balls and Clubs

It is helpful to understand the connection between the ball's design, its trajectory, the club's design, and your swing. If you understand how these relate to each other, you will have a greater chance of creating consistency in your motions and results.

The dimples on the ball, combined with the loft of the club, help project the ball into the air and keep it in the air. The swinging down and through of the clubhead actually pinches, or traps, the ball against the clubface in the grass. The high point in the dimple catches in the grooves of the club when you hit downward and creates a back-spinning motion of the ball. The backspin forces the ball to travel up the clubface and outwards.

Golf clubs today are designed to create what is known as a trampoline effect. The clubface is very thin and it actually moves backwards, or compresses, and then springs forward to push the ball up and outwards.

Your swing motion will change as you progress through the clubs. The sand wedge through the 5 iron have more loft angle and your swing will have more of a hitting downward motion. Conversely, longer clubs have less loft angle. With the 4 iron through the woods, you will use more of a sweeping motion because the club is longer and you are standing further away from the ball. The longer the club, the more clubhead speed is created, and the further the ball travels.

Everyone should be professionally fitted for their clubs, unless they are a beginner. As a beginner, you will not have a repeatable swing and a professional fitting won't make much of a difference in your play. Just start out with a beginner set for ladies or men, with standard flex and length.

When you reach a point that you have a more repeatable swing, you can then be fitted for both irons and woods. As your game improves, this will make a huge difference. At this point, the shaft will be fitted, as is the flex of the shaft, the length, and the lie angle.

The goal of using proper equipment is to maximize your experience. Whether it is to hit the ball further, gain more control, develop more clubhead speed through the hitting area, or get a better feel, every golf manufacturer claims to have the answer. As a player of the game, each individual should call upon him or herself to maximize their skills. Take a lesson. Learn to strike the ball correctly. Practice! Groove your swing for repeated success.

You can have the best equipment and apparel but if you don't have the necessary skills to make it work, you are not maximizing your potential. The role of equipment is to help you, but the equipment cannot do it all alone.

Chapter 5:
An Introduction to the Fundamentals

Fundamentals in golf are essential. If you have not mastered the basics, you will never reach your true potential. You will reach a point that you are playing to the utmost of your natural ability and it will end there. But you can go further than this. Learn the fundamentals correctly, and as you play and practice you will see vast improvement. The sky will be the limit.

Over time, most golfers will intentionally or unintentionally make changes to their game to compensate for bad habits and poor shots. These defensive moves are attempts to just get the ball around the golf course. If you are simply trying to move the ball around the course, this is not the most effective or enjoyable way to play. Go back and learn or relearn the fundamentals; you will be much less frustrated and exponentially more satisfied with your game.

The layout of this book is very straightforward. Each chapter will build upon the skills you learned in the last. We will start with your grip, your posture, alignment, and stance. Then we will discuss putting, chipping, sand play, and the full swing. I will show you how to successfully transition from the practice tee to the golf course. Finally, we will conclude with specialty shots and when and how to use them.

We will break down the game into manageable components and work in incremental steps. This helps to ensure your success even when a golf instructor is not present. Our goal is to create predictable, repeatable actions and results. You will experience breakthrough moments in which you succeed in ways you never have before!

Expect to practice each fundamental multiple times before it feels natural and works. Because you are reteaching your body what to do it will feel awkward at first. Your body will adapt because it will recognize and respond to the fact that what you are doing is correct. I tell you this for two reasons: so you won't be discouraged at the beginning and so you can watch for the progressive improvements.

Don't put too much pressure on yourself to make big improvements in a short period of time. Unrealistic expectations can lead to frustration. Instead, establish workable goals for the ensuing golf season. Set yourself up for success by starting with a few short-term goals that can be met in a reasonable length of time, approximately 6 weeks or less. Start small, this will give you confidence and you will most likely exceed your expectations. After you have successfully met your goals, you can set your sights on some new ones.

I would encourage you to not jump straight to the chapters in this book you are most interested in, as each chapter builds upon skills learned in the last. I am certain that once you get started, you will learn something in every chapter, and you will not want to skip anything.

Chapter 6:
The Grip

We'll start with your grip on the club. If your hands are not placed on the club correctly, you are in for a lot of disappointment as you play. Let's get it right, so you do not have to relearn. Relearning is a pain in the neck, or lower, if you wish.

<u>Left Hand Placement</u>

1-Your left hand is the leader in the golf swing; it is placed on the club first and at the end of the grip. If you look at your left hand, there is an M in the middle of your palm:

I have a clearly defined M, but this picture will help you find yours.

2- The grip should be placed between the long line of the M that is closest to your fingers and your fingers themselves:

It should not be placed in the fingers themselves, as this will create too much release in the wrist:

If the club is placed in the fingers, it will move too quickly and will lack stability. Your club will not stay on the target line long enough and it will shift to the right or left. You may have a good round or occasionally get lucky, but our goal is for you to put your hands on the club and to square the club at impact to your intended target every time.

Conversely, if you do the opposite and grip too high in the palm towards your wrist, you will create wiggle room. Take a look at your glove. If it has worn spots in the heel of the glove, this is a result of wiggle or movement. We will discuss this further in Chapter 8, "Grip Pressure." If you have wiggle room in your grip, you lose the ability to control the golf club and to square your club at impact. The clubface at impact with the ball will have turned to the left or right of your target.

The end of the grip is resting under the fleshy part of your palm. I call this the heel of your hand:

This placement is very important.

3- Before you wrap your fingers around the club, I have exciting news for you. I believe that Ben Hogan had two secrets, not just one. The first he divulged in Life Magazine in 1957, which was the opening of the clubface combined with the supination of the hands. We will discuss the supination of the hands in Chapter 18, "The Full Swing".

His second, I believe unrevealed secret, has to do with the grip and the left hand placement. I was watching an old recording of Hogan and here is what jumped out at me. He had a club in his hands. He took the fleshy part at the base of the left thumb and wrapped it *over* the club.

Most people just hold the club. Hogan deliberately wrapped the fleshy part over the club, so that it was on top of the fingertips. Notice the base of the thumb placing pressure on the fingertips:

I experimented with this and it is phenomenal. This technique locks the grip in place and it is absolutely incredible how much more power you gain. You just don't see people do this. I watched the video a few times and noticed that while it looked like he was just fiddling with the club, every time he placed the fleshy part of the thumb over the club, he smiled right at the camera. He did this three or four times and smiled each time because this was his secret weapon, in my opinion.

4- Just like Hogan, wrap your fingers around the club and lock them in place with the fleshy part at the base of the thumb. The left thumb will be on the right side of the shaft as you look down at your hand:

5 - When you lower your arm, this will put the V that is formed between your thumb and forefinger of the left hand pointed diagonally to your right shoulder:

By placing the left hand in this manner, you will have leverage at the top of your swing to pull the club back down. This will feel uncomfortable at first, but this leverage is very important.

If you do not have the correct V formation in your hand, you will lack the leverage to pull the club down from the top of the backswing. Instead, you will throw it with your right hand, which is your dominant side. The shaft will go straight and you will have no clubhead speed or torquing motion of the shaft. When the torque is dissipated, you will have to force, or push, the swing through with your right hand and arm in an upward motion. This will create topspin instead of backspin. You could also end up creating a slicing motion or a hooking motion. At that point the club will actually go outside the flight line or too far inside the flight line. We will be discussing the flight line in Chapter 10, "Alignment."

If you end up throwing the club with your right hand as described, your odds of striking the golf ball accurately will decrease significantly and the majority of the time it will go to the right. This exact mistake is where many people, especially amateurs, lose a lot of clubhead speed.

If, however, you have the correct V formation as pictured, you will have the leverage to pull the club down with your left hand. The shaft *bows* or flexes, creates torque and stores clubhead speed, and when it releases through impact with the ball, it maximizes the acceleration rate of the clubhead. You will be able to square your club at the intended target and give speed to the club for maximum distance. It seems much easier to do it correctly, doesn't it?

We are looking to create consistency. This can be as simple as confirming the V formation with your thumb and forefinger in your left hand pointed to your right shoulder.

6- The back of your left hand mirrors the clubface so it needs to be square:

This creates stability and keeps the clubhead square for a fraction of a second longer and gives you a more consistent shot pattern.

7- At this point, if you are gripping the club correctly in your left hand you will be able to form a fulcrum with the forefinger and heel of your hand. No other fingers will be on the club when you conduct this check. The club will rest under the heel of the left hand and forefinger:

If the club rolls out of this position you do not have the club far enough under the heel of the hand.

<u>Right Hand Placement</u>

The right hand is the power and it fits behind and underneath the left. Many people incorrectly believe that you need to swing hard, but it's the speed of the swing that creates power. It's not how hard you swing but how fast.

If you place your right hand on the club correctly, you will be able to use all the power you have and hit the ball towards your intended target. Your hands will not fight each other, they will work together in the swing, and you will maximize your clubhead's speed and distance.

1-Look at the palm of your right hand, you will see where the fingers join the hand:

2- Now place your right hand behind and underneath the left. Put the grip in the bottom portion of your fingers, where they connect with the palm, and position your middle two fingers:

3- Wrap the rest of your fingers around the club. The V that is formed between the thumb and forefinger of the right hand is directed straight at your chin:

You can position your fingers in a ten-finger grip or an overlap grip or an interlocking grip. Let's review the grip types and their differences next.

Chapter 7:
Grip Types

The difference between the grips is fairly simple. The common grips are: the Overlap Grip, the 10 Full Finger Grip, and the Interlock Grip.

For all grips, the knuckles will line themselves up in a straight line along the shaft, with the exception of the index finger. If your hands and fingers are aligned correctly, they will help create a better and controllable ball flight and will not fight each other during the swing:

As seen from a different angle:

The Overlap Grip

The little finger of the right hand is placed over the index finger of the left:

Some people hook the knuckle of the left index finger to create more stability, which is ok with me if it feels ok to you:

The 10 Full Finger Grip

All 10 fingers on the club are touching each other without overlapping or interlocking. The little finger of the right hand is touching the forefinger of the left:

This grip is great to help you get the feel of releasing the club through impact. When I talk about releasing, I mean that critical moment in which your hands are in the downswing and they *release from the cocked position*, they speed up, and the clubhead is released to swing through impact with the ball. Stated a different way, the centrifugal force of the golf club gets to the point where you can't swing it any further and it releases through the hitting area.

For students who have trouble releasing with their hands, here is a great exercise. Put the ball on a tee, place your feet together, use a 10 Full Finger Grip with your hands slightly apart, and take a full swing without losing your balance. In this stance, the centrifugal force of the club coming down will force your hands to turn through the hitting area correctly. This exercise helps you feel the relationship between your hands and the clubhead, gives you a better feel of the releasing motion, and helps develop your timing of the clubhead moving through the hitting area.

The Interlock Grip

The little finger of the right hand is placed between the forefinger of the left hand and the middle finger:

As seen from the side:

One has to be careful with this grip. It places the hands closer together which is good, but it also gives the right hand more power. Remember that your left hand should be the leader and the dominant hand. Your right hand is the follower and the power. You need to be sure that you are concentrating on the left side.

If you are just starting to play, I would recommend trying each of the three grips. As you gain a feel for the weight of the clubhead swinging back, down, and through, you can pick which grip is most comfortable. You can change grips if you find better success with another grip; it is not set in stone.

Chapter 8:
Grip Pressure

I have found that as one starts to swing, the hands often come apart or lift slightly off of the club. I call this regripping and it happens to almost all new players and can continue uncorrected for a long time. Even low handicappers may have this problem.

You can determine if this is an issue for you by looking at your glove. If there is a worn spot in the heel of your glove, then the club is not being securely held under the heel. The worn spot is created from the friction of your grip pressure changing.

If you don't use a glove, look at your left hand. If you see calluses, you are changing your grip pressure during your swing. It is possible that you are starting with a stronger pressure that is not sustainable. Strive to maintain the same pressure throughout, even if it means starting with less.

If your hands move or come off of the club during the swing, it will be difficult to square the clubhead at impact. Your right hand will try to compensate and force the club to hit the ball. You will lose control of the club and the ball will almost never go towards the target.

You have to apply a certain level of pressure in the hands and it needs to be consistent through the swing. You must maintain the relationship between your hands and the clubhead with no loss of control.

The right palm should place pressure on the left thumb from start to finish. My right hand is open to illustrate the parts of the hand on which we are focusing:

This ensures that your hands work together and will not change grip pressure or come off the club during the swing. The club will stay square and you will not have a regripping problem.

How do you find the right amount of grip pressure? I have found that the necessary grip pressure varies for everyone, just as the swing varies depending on your height, weight, arm length, and strength.

To help find the correct level of grip pressure, take the clubhead in your right hand and just swing the grip back and forth. You won't feel much weight:

Then switch ends. Take hold of the club grip and swing back and forth. Feel the weight of the clubhead, it will be apparent:

Alternate between swinging the head of the club and the grip, and you will feel the difference. You will become aware of the weight in the clubhead throughout the swing so you can apply the correct amount of pressure.

The correct grip pressure allows you to control your hands, and your hands are the only part of your body that touches the club. When you swing the club, you need to feel the clubhead weight and know where it is within the swing, in order to time your release at the intended target.

If you grip too tightly, you won't be able to feel the clubhead weight. It's like clutching a steering wheel so tightly you can't move it.

Lighten up your touch to the point where you can feel the weight without your hands coming off of the grip.

When you have the correct level of pressure you will feel it in the last 3 fingers of the left hand, the middle 2 fingers of right hand, and the right palm on the left thumb. Keep your pressure intact throughout the swing and hold the finish until the ball hits the ground.

Here is the front view, with lines drawn to the last 3 fingers of the left hand and the middle 2 fingers of the right hand, where you will feel the pressure:

Swinging a weighted golf club can give insight into grip pressure and the relationship between your eye/hand coordination and the clubhead. It provides you with the ability to relate to the clubhead through your hands. A weighted club exaggerates the feel of what your body is doing during the swing; it gives you a sense of rhythm and helps you time the swing. This will help you to release the clubhead at impact and to finish the golf swing.

Many people swing and when they hit the ball, their hands will change grip pressure because they are trying to hit *at* the ball instead of swinging *through* the ball. Don't anticipate the club striking the ball, as this will change your grip pressure mid-swing and slow the momentum. If you let that pressure go, you actually let it go before impact, which will turn the clubface and reduce your speed.

Imagine a quarterback who stops his arm motion when he releases the ball; the momentum and speed of the ball will be lost. He does not do this. Instead, his arm is still travelling after the ball is in flight. Swing *through* the ball, and keep your pressure consistent through the finish, so that your clubface stays square.

Chapter 9:
Posture

Let's talk about posture and setting up for your swing.

1-Place your feet even with the outside of your shoulders:

2- Bend from your waist and stick your butt out, keeping your back straight. You want your weight on the balls of your feet, not the heels. This stance is more stable and athletic:

The pelvis is tilted downward with your tail out; the knees are bent and flexed inward. Your back is straight and your head is over the ball.

Many people will try to tuck their pelvis under, this is not correct:

Tucking your pelvis under forces your arms and hands into the hitting area and restricts the use of your legs. It moves your head back and puts your weight at the heels of your feet. This is a very un-athletic, or unstable, position and it is difficult to swing when your body is not stable. This incorrect position also creates topspin, which will make the ball go down, not up.

How do you know if you are in the incorrect position? If you have done a virtual "sit" in position in which you've just moved your pelvis straight down as opposed to backwards, this is not correct. If you are in this sitting position, you won't get as much speed to your swing.

3- The left side of your body will sit higher than your right. This is because the left hand is placed on the club first, with the right hand underneath and placed second. You will see this slight angle in your shoulders and hips:

4-The knees are slightly bent, with pressure down and inward, towards the balls of your feet. This places pressure on the inside of the knees which ties the upper and lower body together, so they are in sync during the swing, moving in unison and not separately:

I know that this feels awkward, but you will get used to it.

When you are in the correct posture, you will have a *sequence of motion,* in which the muscles fire off of each other. One correct motion leads to the next correct motion. We work on the fundamentals to ensure that when you start your swing correctly, you will have this sequence of motion.

For example, the pelvic bone needs to be tilted and facing downwards so that your hips, knees and ankles get a bit of a lateral motion as you swing through the hitting area. This lateral motion helps to create speed. If the pelvic bone is flat or tilted up, you won't get this lateral motion and your body will end up spinning or turning, which will take the clubface off the line too quickly. The longer your clubface stays on the line, the more accurate your shot will be.

There are three things that professionals practice more than anything else: 1) grip, which we have discussed, 2) posture, and 3) alignment, which we will discuss next. You cannot take posture for granted or ignore it. Without good posture, your body will start to create small manipulations and you won't have the correct sequence of motion, which will affect both your accuracy and distance.

Chapter 10:
Alignment

Alignment is vital to the swing; it also gives the most difficulty to players. Without proper alignment, it is impossible to consistently control the ball's travel direction. A majority of all right-handed golfers unknowingly align their club and feet to the right of their intended target. This causes major problems because you are looking one way and trying to hit in a different direction. Chances are the shot will be to the right or pull-hooked left of the target.

We will discuss the alignment of a straight shot first and then we will discuss hook and cut shots in the next chapter. A straight shot is really just an ideal, rarely are there straight shots. But you need to understand the ideology before you start making adjustments to it, like opening or closing your stance to curve the ball's path.

There are four critical lines you need to identify prior to *every* swing, chip, or putt: 1) the square line on the club, 2) the target line, 3) the foot line, which for a straight shot is parallel to the target line, and 4) the shoulder line which is also parallel to the target line.

1- Find the square line on the club

The leading edge, or bottom line, of the clubhhead is the square line and it will be square to your target. Many people will align the top line of the club to the target. This is not correct, because all clubfaces, even putters, have loft. If you use the top line of the club, the clubface will then face left of the target. The square line of the club extends from the heel to the toe:

2- Find the target line

First, identify your target. You should aim past the pin to maximize acceleration and possibly to the right or left if you are trying to give yourself a margin of error. If the pin is on the right side of the green, aim left of the pin to give yourself a wider landing area to ensure that you will at least hit the green. If you can see that there is a left to right wind moving the trees, aim even further to the left because the wind will push the ball to the right.

Then go stand 10 feet behind the ball before taking the address position and draw an imaginary line from the ball to your target. This is your target line, which you can picture as a wall, or plane, that extends as far as you can see behind the ball, through the middle of the clubface and ball, to the target and beyond, from the ground all the way up to the sky.

Choose your favorite color, except green, to visualize the target line. This may seem like a tiny detail, but very skilled golfers have told me that this tip is of great help. If, for example, your favorite color is orange, your mind will be more engaged when picturing an orange line instead of a plain old black line.

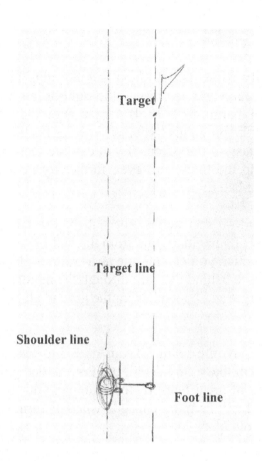

I recommend that you constantly change your target whenever you are on the practice tee. This forces you to reconsider the line with every single swing and will prevent your body from perfecting a bad move.

3- Find the foot line

The foot line is an imaginary line that would be drawn across the tips of your toes. It is to the left of the target line and parallel to it:

Place the sole of the club on the ground so that the square line on the bottom is square to the target. The clubface should face where you want the ball to end up. Then rotate your head back under while looking at the target and place your feet. This is very important. Don't look at the ball and place your feet. Look at the target and *then* place your feet.

By doing this, you engage your Mind's Eye to lock in on the target and to guide your actions appropriately. Your body will be to the left of the golf ball and to the left of your target at address.

4- Find the shoulder line

The shoulder line is fairly self-explanatory, it is an imaginary line drawn from tip to tip of your shoulders. It is also to the left of the target line and parallel to it:

The shoulders should be square to the target, not angled to the right or left. You can see that the left side of your shoulder is higher than the right, which we will discuss in Chapter 13, "Address and Stance."

Your shoulders create the line where your arms and hands are going to swing, so the shoulder line is very important. How do you know if your shoulders are square and parallel to the target line? When you are at address, rotate your head towards your left shoulder. If you don't see your shoulder, then your shoulder is pointed to the left. If this is the case, then turn your shoulders to the right, and rotate your head under (not around) again. You should be able to look over the top of your left shoulder.

If your shoulders are pointed to the left, you will swing outside of the target line and create a left to right shot, or a slice. Conversely, if your shoulders are pointed to the right, your swing will cross the target line, from inside the line to outside and create a right to left shot, or a hook.

If you are not aligned correctly, your subconscious will instinctively realize this and will attempt to compensate by making adjustments to your position and swing. These types of manipulations will slow your clubhead speed, reduce your swinging power and distance, and significantly reduce your chance of building consistency.

5- Check your alignment and ball position with three tees

Take your address position to the intended target and put a tee at your left toe, your right toe, and inside your left heel:

Then step away from the ball and make sure your two parallel lines are in place. You can go behind the ball, to the side, and to the front to check that your ball placement is on the inside of the left heel, which we will discuss in Chapter 13, "Address and Stance:"

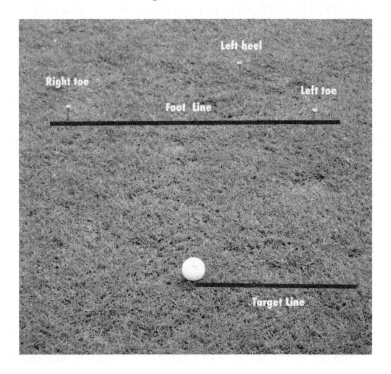

When you practice, you should check your alignment on a regular basis. This will help your swing and ball flight become more consistent.

6- Perfect your eye and head rotation

Your head is the center of the golf swing. It should be behind the ball and over the right knee, with your toes, hips, and shoulders parallel to the target line. If your head is in front of the ball, you won't have any leverage to maximize your clubhead speed.

You can't get the correct stance without the correct rotation of the head. A major flaw of amateur play is that most players have an incorrect eye rotation; they simply look from right to left in a semi-circle on a horizontal plane. Often when they move their head into position, they will inadvertently shift their feet and then they will no longer be parallel to the target line. If your eyes simply rotate from right to left without looking *down and then along* the target line, the feet will end up to the right or left of the line most of the time.

Go behind the ball and draw an imaginary line from the ball, along the ground to the target, and past the target. Pick your favorite color for the line; this will help you to visualize it. When you take the address position, your head and eye rotation should follow that imaginary line. When your head rotates along the line, your left cheek turns towards the sky.

Most players don't think about their eye rotation and instructors largely overlook this. Your head and eyes should move from the right, *down and along the target line,* and then back up to the left to follow the line. This is critical to being aligned correctly and to focusing on your target. Take note, this will be an important step for you in taking your game from the practice tee to the course.

Golf course architects will design the course so that the teeing ground is pointed to the right or left of the fairway, but your eye will not catch this because it's the architect's job to fool you. Go to the back of the teeing area and look down the fairway; you will see where the tee is pointed. If you just walk up to the tee marker, you will not see where the tee is truly pointed. However, if you have the correct eye rotation, you will be fine.

Chapter 11:
Learning and Experimenting with Specialty Shots

Always remember, golf is a game of misses, not a game of perfection. Take the pressure off yourself. When you play, you are learning. Try different things just to see what happens!

I love to experiment. Create different games when practicing: change the targets, hook the ball, or cut the ball so your mind stays engaged. If you experiment on the course, just be courteous of your fellow golfers and do so when fewer people are playing.

Try opening the face of the club to create more loft, and the square line of club will move to the right. Try closing the club and see what happens. Find out for yourself what the ball will do in different situations. Then you will be able to use that information to effectively work around obstacles like trees and bodies of water.

There are 9 shots in golf: straight, low straight, high straight, normal hook, low hook, high hook, normal cut, low cut, and high cut. All good players have a "go to" shot that, under any circumstance, they can hit every time. This is the shot they can always count on under pressure. If at all possible, though, I would encourage you to have a couple of "go to" shots.

During a straight shot, when your club is on the target line, it is actually half on the inside and half on the outside of the line. You do not want your club to go outside the target line unless you are trying to hook or cut the ball.

Most players only know how to do a hook shot or a cut shot, but you really should learn to do both. Then you can take your most strategic shot, the shot that has the best chance of getting to the green in the shortest number of strokes. By knowing how to both hook and cut, you can work the ball away from trouble spots like bunkers and bodies of water and you won't cost yourself extra shots.

In both the hook and the cut shots, the clubface is square to the target and the club will cross the target line. A hook shot will cross the target line from inside to out and a cut shot will cut from out to in.

1- Creating a hook shot

To create a hook, or draw shot, align the clubface to the target and close your stance by moving to the right. The amount to which you close your stance will depend on how much hook you need to create. Practice will help you discover this. Your shoulders will be angled to the right and your left side will be high. Your shoulders and feet will be to the right of the flight line.

Hit the inside corner of the ball, so it will fly from right to left, and make your normal swing. Your arms and hands will swing through and produce a right-to-left spin on the ball because the golf club swings where the shoulders are pointed. The ball will start to the right of the target, "hook" or spin back to the left, and then arrive at the target.

To illustrate, this is normal alignment:

The ball's line of flight is identical to the target line. We've chosen a target line to the flag, but as discussed, you may choose a different target line if you are aiming to give yourself a margin of error on the green.

This is after making the adjustment for a hook shot:

You can turn your left hand to the right to strengthen your grip. This increases the turning motion of the hands through the hitting area to speed up the hands and create more hook:

2- Creating a cut shot

To create a cut, or fade shot, square the clubface to the target and open your stance. Your shoulders and feet will point to the left of the target and to the left of the target line. The degree to which you open to the left depends on the how much cut you need.

This is after making the adjustment to your alignment for a cut shot:

Hit the outside corner of the ball so it will fly from left to right. Your arms and hands will swing through and produce a left-to-right spin on the ball. The ball will start to the left of the target, "cut" or spin back to the right, and then arrive at the target.

You can turn your left hand to the left to weaken your grip, which takes much of the release out of the swing, and increases the level of cut:

The variants of the hook and cut shots are:

3-Creating a low shot

To create a low shot, the ball is positioned back of center towards your right foot. This takes some loft off of the club and the ball will fly lower:

4- Creating a high shot

To create a high shot, the ball is positioned front of center close to the left heel. This creates more loft by opening the clubface:

Move your hands even with the back of the ball, as opposed to in front of the ball as in the Reverse K address position. This sends the ball higher in the air.

Chapter 12:
Your Pre-Game Routine and Pre-Shot Routine

The time to warm up and think about your game and the shots you are going to take is before you play, not after. Too many times, players lament a poor shot after the fact without having ever considered what type of shot they were going to take in the first place.

Your Pre-Game Routine

Begin with your choice of stretching exercises. These help create elasticity in your muscles and more elasticity will generate more club head speed for you. You will have the mobility to turn and load your swing at the top of the backswing.

After stretching, start with the short clubs to warm your muscles up and do a few practice swings. You will always do better after your muscles are loosened up, so do this before your game not during it.

A good warm-up and practice exercise is to swing the club using only one hand at a time. Tee several balls and take the club in the left hand only and strike them. Then do the same using only the right hand. This provides good feedback as to the releasing and feel of each arm and hand during the swing. When you have a better understanding of what each arm and hand does individually, it will be easier for you to swing more effectively when both hands are back on the club together.

Your Pre-Shot Routine

Many golfers do not pay enough attention to their pre-shot routine; they simply hit the ball. Often a swing is taken with no thought as to where the ball is going, how it will get there, or what kind of shot is necessary to produce a good result.

Your pre-shot routine is about how you get into position. Go through the pre-shot routine every time, regardless of what type of shot you are taking: putt, chip, or long shot.

1- Walk eight to ten feet behind the ball so that you can get a true vision of what type of shot you want, i.e., left to right or vice-versa, distance, and target.

2-Indentify your target and your flight line every time. When you stand back to get your flight line, take the time to visualize yourself standing at address, taking the swing, hitting the ball, and holding the finish. Picture the ball's path of travel and its landing. You need to see both the swing and the ball finishing. This only takes a few seconds but it is very important because by using the Mind's Eye to create these images, you will pre-program your body to make the correct shot.

Greg Norman gives the best example of checking the flight line every time. He does his pre-shot routine every time he addresses the ball. When you practice, you should be checking your alignment on a regular basis. This will help to make your swing more consistent and your ball flight more repeatable.

3- Place your right foot first and square the club to your intended target. You must continue to look at the target while rotating your head under and then place your left foot. Don't look back at the ball. This will help you lock in on the target. When you move your head into position behind the ball, rotate it under and not around. This will guarantee that your alignment is pretty close, and it will get better over time.

4- At the address position, hit the shot in your Mind's Eye. Envision the club as it is pushed back. See the club being pulled down from the top of the swing, hitting the ball, and propelling the ball into the air. Envision the ball landing and coming to rest in good position for the next shot. Once you have hit the shot in your Mind's Eye and seen where the ball comes to rest, you have pre-programmed your muscles and they will know what is expected of them.

When you go through the pre-shot routine and envision the shot, do not envision a shot you cannot make. One of the biggest issues golfers encounter is their desire to hit the ball further than they are able with their own skills or with their selected equipment. It is better to swing within your or your equipment's abilities for a reasonable distance than to hit it longer, go off-line, and cost yourself more strokes.

When we talk about envisioning the shot, the swing, the ball's path of travel and landing, we are talking about being in the present and focused on the shot at hand. Getting over a bad shot or hole is difficult, but absolutely essential. Hit one shot at a time and stay focused. Bad shots do and will happen. When you are playing, let the errors go and anticipate the possibility of the next opportunity.

Make the best of what is before you. If your mind races forward to the end of the round, or if negative aspects of the game you've played so far overtake your thoughts, your score will undoubtedly be higher. Emotions will come into play and with that, loss of control. Try to develop good habits and a positive attitude that can't be taken away with one swing of the golf club.

By going through this pre-shot routine, you are preparing your mind and your body to get in the right position. You are telling your muscles that you are getting ready to make a swing. Then walk up and execute!

Chapter 13:
Address and Stance

<u>The K Address</u>

I prefer the K address, as described in the Golf Digest book "Golf Lessons with Mr. X." The left arm and the shaft of the club form a straight line and the right arm and right leg form the other two lines of the K:

1- When you are at address, and before you start the swing, the insides of your elbows will be facing upwards and your arms will be as close together as possible throughout the swing. This will tie the upper arms and body together and they will work as one unit.

2- There should be a slant to the shoulders, with the left side higher than the right. I also like to feel that there is a slight tilt on the right side at my waist. This will put your head behind the ball and in a better position to swing the club outwards and towards the target.

3- Your head is behind the ball, not over it:

If your head is over the ball at address, there is a good chance that you will move forward when you are in the downswing. This can cause any number of problems from slicing to pull-hooking the golf ball.

4- Double-check your grip. You should see at least two knuckles of the left hand at address. This will help ensure that your left hand is strong enough to pull the club down from the top of the swing.

5- Hold the club slightly above the ground. This will help you avoid grounding the club to the soil, which can cause you to change your grip or to grip too tightly. Too much tension in the arms and hands at address will create a quick pulling-away motion from the ball and the transition from the backswing to the downswing will be too fast and jerky.

This is the correct position of the club held slightly above ground:

Hold the club lightly without changing grip pressure and the first part of the swing will be much smoother, allowing the finished shot to maximize its potential.

6- Your hands are even with the front side of the ball that is facing the target, or just ahead of it, so that you are not creating angles in the long line of the K.

7- The back of your elbows should be pointed down or towards your hips. You want to *push* the club back with the top left shoulder muscle, not just pick it up. The club will stay in plane and online longer through impact, which will lead to better ball flight and straighter shots.

Here is a front view with the elbows pointed down, arms close together, and hands even with the front side of the ball:

8- Check your position. There are 2 checks to ensure that you are in the correct position.

The left hand should be on the inside of the left thigh and the hosel will be in your direct line of sight right before the ball. When you look at the golf ball with your right eye, your line of sight will cross at the hosel of the club, and not higher, on the shaft:

Stance:

With shorter clubs, the ball will be farther from the left heel and more towards the center of the stance; longer clubs are the opposite. Make sure that the ball is not past your heel towards your instep or this will cause a fade or a pull-hook.

To help you determine your stance for the irons and woods, I will provide several examples from short through long clubs, starting with the sand wedge. As you progress from the sand wedge through the driver, the ball position will only move 2 to 2.5 inches from the left heel, no more than that.

1- Starting with the sand wedge, the ball is placed back in the stance off the inside of the left heel by 2 inches:

Your goal with this iron is for the ball to go high and land soft.

2- With the 8 iron, your stance is not as open and the ball is a shade farther forward. The ball is placed back in the stance off the left heel by about 1.5 inches but everyone is different, so you don't need to actually measure. The left side is open to the target a bit:

3-With the 6 iron, the ball is forward even a bit more. With the 4 wood, the ball is even farther forward. And so on. Remember that as you progress from the sand wedge through to the driver, the ball position will only move 2 to 2.5 inches from the left heel.

4- Here are examples of the stance for the sand wedge, 7 iron, 5 iron, 3 iron, 3 wood, and the driver.

The sand wedge:

The 7 iron:

The 5 iron:

The 3 iron:

The 3 wood:

The driver:

Now that we have confirmed your stance for the irons and the woods, let's move on to hitting balls!

The Short Game

Chapter 14:
Scoring is 100 Yards and In

If you want to make the most immediate impact to your game, focus on the short game. Sixty to seventy percent of your game will be played 100 yards and in. Practice putting, chipping, and sand play to lower your score. At 100 yards or less, your chance of improving your overall score improves by leaps and bounds; the long game is just harder to impact.

Around the green, from ten to fifteen yards, there are many different shots you can learn to play. I always try to let the loft of the club do the work for me. The loft of the club propels the ball so you don't have to change your chip swing, just change your club. It's easy!

Let's say you are ten yards short of the green and the flag is on the back of the green and the green is sloped against you. Instead of playing the same old shot that you have been using for years with the sand wedge or pitching wedge, choose a club that will let the loft work for you.

Try a 6 or 7 iron to chip the ball one-third of the way to the hole and let the ball roll the remaining two-thirds of the way. When the ball rolls upon landing, it will behave like a putt and follow the contours of the green. Chances are good that the ball will stop closer to the pin than it would have with the shot you normally take.

A lot of people get "one club happy." They do themselves a disservice and, by using the same club every time, turn a simple shot into a hard shot. People love using the driver, but that's not the scoring club. The putter and your chipping clubs are the ones that will help improve your score.

Let's get started with your short game.

Chapter 15:
Putting Basics

Putting is the most individual part of the golf game. Many people will develop their own techniques and choice of putter that is both comfortable for them and repeatable. But before you start to customize your putting technique, ensure that you understand the basics of putting.

The putt is the only shot in golf with topspin, or over-spin, on the ball. Topspin will create distance but will help your ball hold the line by digging into the green and moving towards the hole. All putters have loft to help produce topspin; most have about three or four degrees of loft.

1- The upper arms and elbows are held in tight to the sides of your body, which creates a connected feeling and a solid strike:

There should be no independent motion of the wrists. I prefer a heavier putter so you can feel the stroke more, especially for beginners.

A heavier putter will help you feel the relationship between the putter head and your hands, arms, and shoulders moving together as one unit.

2- Remember that the left hand is the leader. The back of the left hand faces your target, as does the palm of the right hand, even though your fingers are closed and the palm is hidden.

Ensure that you are holding the putter correctly. If you open your right fingers and thumb, the palm should be facing the target. If you open your left fingers and thumb, the left palm should be facing your right palm:

Then close your hands as you normally would:

Your hands are parallel to each other when they are placed on the club so they work together. They should be in front of the ball, not behind it.

3- It is critical to ensure that your head doesn't move. The head is slightly behind, not over, the putter and the ball and you will be looking at the backside of the ball:

4- Position your weight on your left side, this helps to anchor you so you won't move during the putt.

5- The ball is played off the inside of the left heel and the left wrist is arched so that your wrist doesn't break down through impact:

The following is not correct; note the left wrist is not arched and is behind the ball:

6- The toe of the putter is flat on the ground and the heel of the putter will be slightly above the ground. Many people will place their hands too low with the toe of the putter off the ground, which is not correct. The toe of the putter flat on the ground will help ensure that the slight arch in your left wrist doesn't break down at impact:

7- If you are using a face-balanced putter, the face of the club will face the ground when it reaches the back of the stroke:

Beginners should start with a center-shafted putter so they don't have to worry about where to strike the ball. Play the ball at the center of shaft and you will get more feedback as to solidness of the stroke.

8- You want a smooth, short stroke. If your stroke is too long, you will have a tendency to decelerate the putter through impact. When you decelerate the putter, two things happen: the putter blade may wobble which makes it hard to hold the line and it becomes hard to judge your distance.

For a putt approximately 10 feet or less, the backstroke is only about 6 inches but the putter blade will be well past 6 inches on the follow through. This varies by the length of the putt, a short putt may only be 6 inches but a longer putt will be more.

Develop a putting stroke that goes back slowly and then accelerates, so there is no movement in your grip, and the ball will roll with topspin. To help you develop a smooth and accelerated stroke, take the grip off of your center-shafted putter, fill the shaft with sand, replace the grip, and practice a bit. This also helps you engage the big muscles and big muscles create the smooth movements we are striving for.

9- Keep your head down in position after you have hit the putt for a second or two. This will help your putt stay on the line that you chose.

10- Always practice outside. We are working on your eyes, hands, sense of feel, and understanding how these relate to the grass and contours of the green. You will not get the same experience if you use an inside putting matt. Practice, practice, practice! Don't get too bogged down with mechanics. You are building up your level of experience and developing your awareness of your senses and feel.

Chapter 16:
Putting Distance and Distance Control

There are two essential components to understand when putting: distance control and direction. Of these two, distance control is more important. To address this, practice with your eyes shut.

If you close your eyes when practicing long putts, listen for the sound of the ball dropping into the hole. Hearing the time lag helps you get a feel for time and distance travelled.

Take a long iron and place it about 18 inches behind the hole so that if you miss, you will still hear the ball hit something. This gives your brain an idea of how much to accelerate the club for a particular length of putt.

I'd rather you aim to putt past the hole as opposed to short of it. A putt that is short of the hole has zero chance of going in, but if you are aiming to go past the hole, you have at least given yourself the opportunity to make the putt.

I also encourage students to practice with their eyes closed in order to get feel of the motion for certain distance putts. This really helps people with a touch problem; it gives them feedback as to the relationship between their hands and the putter head. You need to have a feel for the weight of the clubhead in order to know where it is in the stroke.

When your eyes are shut, you will start envisioning everything. This helps bring your conscious and subconscious minds together. Our goal is to make your subconscious come alive and get with the program.

Here is a great exercise I learned at a PGA Nationals playing workshop. It will improve your confidence in your short putt and your ability to roll the ball. Stand at the cup on a putting green and pretend the cup is in the middle of the clock. Walk three feet and place a tee in that spot. This is 12 o'clock. Go back to the cup and walk three feet to place a tee at 3 o'clock, 6 o'clock, and 9 o'clock respectively:

You now have four tees placed three feet from the cup. Pick one of the spots you've marked with your tee. Take three golf balls and putt all of them from that spot:

When you make all three putts in a row, move to the next tee. If you miss a putt, go back to the beginning. Once you have made all three putts at all four locations, move the tees back another foot from the cup. When you can make all of these putts, move the tees to five feet. There are 36 putts in all. It's amazing how effective this drill is.

Chapter 17:
Putting Direction

If the green is contoured, pick a spot to aim for in which you believe the ball will turn, or break, and then head back to the hole. Let the green move the ball for you, using the slope of the land and the grass grain direction. Knowing exactly where to aim is a matter of practice and experience. Stand on the green and pick different spots to aim for and watch where the ball breaks. Try different putts just to see what happens!

When you walk up to the green, notice which way the contours of the land. Ask yourself "if it rained, where would the water drain off the green?" This will give you an idea of which direction the ball will break:

You need to consider both the slope of the land and the grain of the grass. Bermuda grass normally leans towards the setting sun. If you look at the grass and it looks dull, you are looking against the grain. If it looks shiny, then you are with the grain. If you are putting with the grain of the grass, the ball will turn faster than against the grain.

Stand behind the ball and envision the putt. If you have a right to left putt, or a left to right, also go to the low side of the ball and look at the slope. Then go behind the ball again and reenvision the putt. View the putt from the back and from the side to ensure that you understand the angle and severity of the land's slope and contours.

Pick your favorite color (not green) to picture a line on the grass that will be the ball's path. This helps to communicate to your subconscious what you want it to accomplish.

Experiment! If the ball didn't follow the path you had intended, try envisioning a different path.

Chapter 18:
Chipping, Pitching, and the Wrist Cock Shot

You should start with a chip when you are about thirty feet from the pin just off the green. Many people will putt from just off the green; I don't recommend this because there could be hidden bumps under the grass, which will throw your ball offline. I prefer to get the ball over the fringe area instead of through it. If you are in higher grass, you will need more loft to get the ball up and over to land on the green and to let it roll. You want to get the ball onto the green as soon as possible, so that it will follow the contours of the putting surface.

There are two basic types of chipping: chipping and pitching and chipping with a wrist cock. We will discuss both and the circumstances under which you use each.

Chipping and Pitching

The chip becomes a pitch when you are around thirty to eighty yards from the green and using the pitching or sand wedge. Chipping and pitching are like putting in that you hold your upper arms close to your body.

1-Apply pressure between the inside of your arms and your chest. This ties everything together and your upper body will work together as a unit:

2- In setting up for a chip or pitch, the hands are ahead of the clubhead and ball for all shots:

If your hands are behind the clubhead, you will have a tendency to flip the shot, which causes the club to go up through the hitting area. This, in turn, creates topspin which will make the ball go down not up:

3- You want your weight on the left side to anchor you. This helps you to strike down and through the shot.

4- Don't neglect your pre-shot routine. Walk up to ten feet behind the ball so you can determine what type of shot you will need. In your Mind's Eye, envision the ball's flight line in your favorite color. See the ball's path and its landing. Picture your swing and finish.

5- You should be looking at the back of the ball when you strike it. The back of the ball actually has three sides: the center, the outside, and the inside. When putting and chipping, you are looking at and striking the center of the back of the ball.

6- There is a descending motion in the stroke. The downward motion of the club creates backspin by pinching the ball against the clubface, sending the ball up against the grooves on the face, and propelling the ball up and outward. The backspin allows you to control the ball.

7- Depending on length of the shot needed, take the club back a certain distance and then forward a certain distance. Finish the shot with the same amount on the backswing as the follow through. You want to get the ball on the green and let it run the rest of the way. Your clubface will always face the target at the finish.

When you are chipping, you are not trying to make the ball go a long way. In order to be relatively good around the green, let the loft of the club do the work for you. Your club selection will depend on where the pin is and where you are in relation to it. If the pin is close to you, use a more lofted club. The closer you are to the pin, the more loft you want. This will get the ball higher in the air; it will land softly and not roll too far.

If the pin is close to you and you don't have much green to work with, you can use a sand wedge or 60-degree wedge. This will create enough loft for the ball to land softly on the green and come to a rest. If the pin is further away, use a less lofted club. I have used a 4 iron to chip with, if the circumstances are right.

If you need the ball to land softer, weaken the left hand grip just a shade. If you are looking at the top of the grip, turn your left hand to the left a bit. You will need to practice and fiddle with this a bit in order to perfect this technique.

This is before making the adjustment:

This is after making the adjustment to weaken the left hand:

Chipping Examples:

1-Thirty foot chip with a 7 iron

Chip it 1/3 of the way and let the ball roll the other 2/3 of the way so it follows the contour of the green. By doing so, you will have a better chance of getting the ball close to the hole.

2-Thirty foot chip uphill with a 5 or 6 iron

Use the same stroke as you would with the 7 iron, but use a 5 iron to let the loft of the club work for you. The 5 iron has less loft than the 7 iron and will keep the ball lower to the ground and moving faster. When it lands, the ball will have more steam so it will have an easier time running up the hill.

Pitching Examples:

1-Thirty yard pitch with a pitching wedge

If you are 30 yards from the green and the pin is at the back of the green, use a pitching wedge to get the ball on the green so it runs to the hole. The pitching wedge has less loft than the sand wedge; it will hit the green and run more instead of coming to a halt.

2- Thirty yard pitch with a sand wedge

If you are 30 yards from the green and the pin is close to you, use a sand wedge to get the ball up quickly, it will not roll as far when it lands.

The Wrist Cock Shot

You may need to use a wrist cock shot for a variety of reasons. For example, if there is a tree behind you and you can't fully extend your arms, use a wrist cock shot to keep the ball in play.

When you are 10 to 15 feet away from the green with the pin close to the edge of the green, you need to get the ball up quickly to land softly and come to a rest. To do so, you will need to adjust your loft and use a wrist cock.

The flop shot is a wrist cock shot that everyone should have in his or her arsenal. You will lay the clubface open to increase the loft. The degree to which you open the face is determined by how much loft you need.

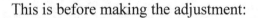

This is before making the adjustment:

This is after opening the clubface:

After opening the clubface, execute the flop shot with a quick wrist cock, or a hinging motion of the wrist as you swing back:

The steeper the angle to your wrist cock, the softer and shorter the ball will come out. Use a sand shot but hit the ball directly, instead of behind the ball, in a down-and-through motion. The follow through on the swing will be the same length as the backswing.

If you need to, you can soften the ball's landing by turning your left hand to the left to weaken the grip. This will encourage the ball to come to rest when it lands instead of running.

In general, as the pin gets closer to you, the more your wrists will play a part. When the pin is further away, you will use the big muscles of your arms and shoulders. The club will swing back and through, which we will discuss in Chapter 20, "The Full Swing." Before we move onto the full swing, though, let's discuss the final shot in the short game, which is the bunker shot.

Chapter 19:
Sand Play Around the Green

A lot of people fear the bunker shot, but it is the easiest shot in golf because you aren't trying to strike the ball itself. You are striking an inch to an inch and a half behind the ball, allowing the sand to push the ball up and out. You don't have to be as exact as in other shots.

The key to this shot is to finish the swing. If you stop once the club hits the sand, the ball won't go anywhere.

Here are a few types of bunker shots you will encounter and how to execute them.

<u>The Regular Bunker Shot, Splash Shot, or Explosion Shot:</u>

This is a u-shaped swing in which the club crosses the target line. You are actually making a cut swing with the sand wedge, which starts outside the target line, comes down, and cuts across to inside the line.

1- Because you are making a cut shot, your body is well open to the target. You will need to take into account that the ball will come out a little to the right, so align yourself more to the left of the target line.

Stand with the left side of your body opened to the target and play the ball on the inside of the left heel. Your weight is on the left side, to encourage a downward motion to the swing.

Because this is a short bunker shot, the flight line is straight; it does not have time to curve from left to right.

Here is a view from behind the ball:

Here is the front view, note the ball position at the inside left heel and the flight line which mirrors the target line:

2- You need a lot of loft so use the sand wedge, or a 56% to 60% wedge. Open the clubface and take it outside the line of flight to the top of the backswing.

3- Start the swing with a very sharp wrist cock, or hinge, upward; the steeper the angle, the softer and shorter the ball will come out:

4- When the club is at the top of the swing, let the weight of the club head drop down and hit 1 to 1.5" behind the ball:

5- Let the club slide beneath the ball. Don't dig deep, stay just under the surface. If you were drinking a cup of coffee or a glass of soda, and a bug was on the surface, you would take a spoon and skim the top, not go to the bottom of the drink and come up from there to retrieve the bug.

The technique of sliding the club under the ball also works around the green and in the rough to make the ball come out softer. If you do this in the grass, the only difference is that your club will catch the ball first, as opposed to the sand.

6- Do not release the hands when you follow through, instead, hold with both hands. The face of the club will end up facing the target. Don't let the club turn left of the target. This is what I call a hold finish, not a full release finish. Your hands will stop at the 8 or 9 o'clock position, as opposed to completing a full swing:

The sand will push the ball up and out and will give the ball spin. Some people like to call this a Splash Shot. I call it an Explosion Shot. As with other iron shots, this shot has a downward motion, the only difference is that you are hitting behind the ball and not hitting the ball itself. The sand pushes the ball up and out. You will see a shallow divot in the sand; it is not deep:

The Ball Half-Buried Bunker Shot:

If the ball is half buried in the sand, you will need to change a few tactics.

1- Your body weight will be more evenly distributed and not as much on the left side as in a regular bunker shot.

2- Like the Explosion Shot, you need the loft of the sand wedge. But the clubface will be square as opposed to open:

3- You will use the same motion with a quick wrist cock, but use a hold finish to hit and hold at impact because the ball is going to come out very fast, with no spin on it. If the ball only needs to travel a short distance, stop your hands at 6:00. If the ball needs to travel further, hit and hold to 7:00 or 8:00. The sand will elevate the ball up and out:

You will notice that the divot is deeper than in a regular bunker shot:

The Fairway, or Long, Bunker Shot:

This is, in my opinion, the hardest shot in golf with a pitching wedge. Anything longer than 30 yards requires a lot more touch sensitivity and a lot more practice.

When you swing, you will have two goals. The first is to stay calm from the waist down so your feet don't slip. The second is to make contact with the ball first before the sand, unlike the Explosion Shot.

1-When you are in the sand and you take your stance, wiggle your feet down so you anchor yourself and avoid slippage during the swing. Then stay calm from the waist down.

Your club won't have as much speed as it would if you were standing on grass because there can be very little weight transfer in your lower body with this shot. If normally you would use a 7 iron, use a 6. If you are facing into the wind, use a 5.

2- Your second goal is to catch the ball first as opposed to the sand. Play the ball center or right of center; this places the ball in a position where it is easier to catch the ball first:

Once you catch the ball you can swing through. You can use a sand wedge for 50 to 80 yard bunker shots, after 80 yards you will start to use the pitching wedge, 9 iron, 8 iron, and so forth as the distance gets longer. Use a long iron or a wood for the fairway bunker shot:

This shot is no different than if you are in the fairway, but in this circumstance you are standing on an unstable surface. You will not be able to hit the ball as far as you normally would. The tips I have provided will help you maximize the distance you can achieve in these conditions.

Always leave the course better than you found it; this includes bunkers too:

The Long Game

Chapter 20:
The Full Swing

To maximize your full swing, focus on using the big muscles, not the little ones. Big muscles create long, smooth movements and little muscles create fast, jerky movements. If you start with the use of small muscles, they will be engaged throughout the whole swing and this is not what you want.

The shoulders are very important to a powerful full swing. There are two rotations to pay attention to. When you push the club back and turn your shoulders in the backswing, the first rotation is the shoulders moving *around*. Then as the downswing starts, the left shoulder moves up and the right shoulder moves down and underneath the chin. This is the second rotation. The entire sequence is around, then down, and under for the right shoulder.

The Backswing

1- Take a couple of trial swings with your eyes closed and feel the club being pushed back with the top outside of your left shoulder muscle. This is the first shoulder rotation. You are not jerking it back with your right hand and wrist. Closing your eyes will sharpen your senses and help you to identify the correct muscle area.

2- You want width in your swing, so the back left quadrant will be stretched. When you are at address and ready to start the backswing, push back with your left arm and extend your arms as far back as they will go. This stretches the muscle, and like a spring, tightens and loads it for release. The more you can stretch that muscle, the more clubhead speed you will generate. This is very important.

Here is the stretched back left quadrant, where you should feel the stretch:

Remember the phrase, "Wider is tighter." The more width you have in your golf swing, the tighter or more controlled it will be. If you hinge your hands and bend your left elbow, your arms will be loose. Extend your arms and this will tighten up your swing.

3- As you push the club back at the start of the backswing, the club should be on the foot line when it reaches hip height:

If the club is inside the foot line when it reaches your right hip height, your swing will be off plane:

4- When your arms are extended as far back as they will reach, the right elbow needs to be pointed downwards not out:

The Top of the Backswing

1- At the top of the backswing, your weight is ninety percent on the inside of your right leg and ten percent on the inside of your left front foot. You will roll a bit on the inside of the left toe and the left heel is off the ground:

2- Your right knee stays flexed; it does not straighten:

Your feet are touching the ground; use this connection and the flex in your knee to power your legs and feet. Imagine if we suspended your body a couple of inches off the ground, you would not be able to use your feet. Stay flexed and use the ground to push off of when you shift the weight in your feet.

Many amateurs will straighten their right knee when they reach the top of the backswing and then they lack power in their lower body:

If the right knee is straightened and locks, you will throw the club from the top downwards and outside the flight line. This dissipates the shaft flex and causes the clubhead to lose speed. If your legs are locked, you have completely taken them out of the picture.

3- Your upper body is coiled; your back is turned to the target. Note the raised left heel:

Feel the stretch in the upper left side of your back. All the speed and power will come from your legs and stretched back left shoulder muscle. Remember that loaded spring.

4- Many will over-swing and allow the club to drop behind their back. When this happens, the player will throw their arms and club outwards on the downswing and will lose the shaft flex that is critical to the speed and accuracy of the shot.

Shorten your swing so that the club does not drop behind your back. When you feel pressure on the left thumb at the top of the swing, it is time to stop the backswing:

5- Know where your clubhead is during the swing. In Chapter 8, we discussed the relationship between your hands and the clubhead and maintaining the correct grip pressure. You need to feel the clubhead weight in order to know when it is at the top of the backswing and when the downward part of the swing begins.

If your swing is too fast, you won't sense the completion of the backswing and the start of the downswing. It will be a blur and your control will go right out the window. Take your swing to the top and pause for a split second, so you know when to start the downswing.

Tempo and balance go hand in hand in the golf swing. Without these, the swing does not work properly. Someone who pushes the club back too quickly will not be able to swing through the hitting area with the same speed. It will be slower than the backswing.

More often than not, when the club is pushed back too fast, your balance will shift to the left foot. This is a reverse transfer of body weight, commonly referred to as a "reverse pivot." The "reverse pivot" causes a range of issues like topping the ball, slicing, and not hitting the ball solidly.

Hold the club lightly enough to be able to feel the clubhead moving both back and through. Practice by swinging the club to the top of the backswing and coming to a complete stop. Then swing the club to a complete follow-through. Do this several times and you will learn good tempo and balance.

6- Pull the club back down with your body weight transferring simultaneously. When you took the backswing, your body weight and the club moved in the same direction and your body weight was ninety percent on the inside of your right knee. When you swing back down, your weight shifts to the left side before release.

The Downswing

When you gripped the club before you took the swing, you formed the correct V formation in the left hand that we discussed in Chapter 6, "The Grip." The V that is formed between your thumb and forefinger points diagonally to your right shoulder, and gives you the leverage to pull the club down from the top of the backswing.

1- As you begin the downswing, you will transfer your weight in your feet while simultaneously dropping your arms and hands down. If your right knee stays flexed, you can brace on the inside of your right lower leg. Your knees are pointed inwards and down, as if riding a horse:

Push off of your inner right foot and shift your weight to your left side. It is a simultaneous motion as you transfer your weight and your arms drop down towards the hitting area, but the sequence starts in your feet and then moves up through your body.

2- As your arms drop down, the left shoulder moves up, and the right shoulder moves down and underneath the chin. This is the second shoulder rotation that we discussed at the beginning of this chapter:

3- As the downward motion of the golf swing begins, the swing should start slowly and build as the club nears impact. Let the speed build naturally. The player who does this will have more consistent shots and lower scores. Be a swinger of the golf club, not a hitter of the golf ball.

Many amateur players try to increase their swing speed by moving their legs and feet too fast. This causes the lower body to move ahead of the upper body, with the top part having to play catch-up, which is not proficient. The club cannot stay on the target line long enough for you to actually align the ball to the target.

An easy way to prevent the lower body from moving too fast is to keep your right foot or heel on the ground until the ball has been struck. Then let the foot come up and finish the shot with the right toe on the ground, heel in the air, chest and stomach facing the target, and weight on the left side.

4- As you are pulling the club down, you will reach a point where your arms and hands are dropped down and the right and left hands will be cocked:

5- Your hands will release from the cocked position, the back of the left hand will be square to the target, and you will finish your swing as the hands rotate through the hitting area. You should feel that you have hit the ball with the back of the left hand, which mirrors the clubface.

Many people have difficulty achieving the correct hand action through impact. They try to shove the club through the hitting area and never achieve the proper amount of clubhead speed. The more the player tries, the worse it gets.

You should feel the left hand pull down towards the ball. As the clubhead approaches the ball, the hands will start to turn. You will feel that the left palm is going to *turn upwards through impact*. This will release your hands, and square the clubhead at the same time towards the target. In this way, you will achieve maximum clubhead speed.

You can practice a baseball swing in preparation for the golf swing. This helps increase the rotation of your hands and arms, which will increase the clubhead speed and release. Ben Hogan referred to this as the supination of the hands through the hitting area. Fully rotate your hands and wrists through the hitting area:

Here's a great way to ensure that you are fully supinating: put your feet together and separate your hands on the club and then swing. This forces your hands to supinate and release through the hitting area. You will literally fall over if you don't supinate.

<u>Finishing the Swing</u>

All touring professionals finish their swing and hold the finish until the ball hits the ground. They do this for three reasons: 1) to develop consistency of motion and shot pattern, 2) to maintain their balance, and 3) to maximize clubhead speed. The clubhead moves through the hitting area the same way every time, with no slowing or distortion. Take a tip from them and follow their example.

Finishing the swing helps you to maintain grip pressure at the end, but don't forget to keep your grip pressure consistent throughout the swing. Swing through the ball, not at it, so that your grip pressure will not distort, and your clubface will stay square.

Many players have a recoil. They swing and jerk back, which slows the clubhead before impact, and they will never reach maximum clubhead speed. I recommend that you swing a weighted club 20 times in the morning and 20 times in the evening to help counter this impulse.

When you have the correct level of pressure you will feel it in 3 different points: the last 3 fingers of the left hand, the roots of the middle 2 fingers of the right hand, and the right palm on the left thumb. Don't manipulate the club with the index finger, as many people do. Keep your pressure intact throughout the swing and hold the finish until the ball hits the ground.

Chapter 21:
Taking it from the Practice Tee to the Golf Course

There are three things that professionals practice more than anything else: 1) grip, 2) posture at address, and 3) alignment. They know that if these three things are in place when they swing the club, their chances of success are much greater. If you are having issues transitioning from the practice tee to the course, one of these items is not right.

To check if you are gripping the club correctly, ensure that the palm of your right hand faces the target, as does the back of your left hand. You should see at least two knuckles of the left hand at address.

Poor posture won't allow you to make the same swing every time and you need to have control over your swing. Make sure that your left side of the body is higher than the right. Look at your ball placement. Ensure that your ball is not too far forward. If it is, this will cause a fade or cut.

Most players who don't transition well have incorrect alignment. If you are not aligned to the target, your body will subconsciously make an adjustment in the swing to get the ball back to the target. These types of adjustments cause unpredictability and loss of control.

Make the most of your time on the practice tee. Go through all the same steps you do when you are on the course. Take time to identify your target. Don't bang out balls at the same target every time, you could be teaching your body to perfect an incorrect move. You may be getting it right on the practice tee because your mind and body keep repeating the same manipulations to hit the same target, but it won't work on the course. There are just too many variables.

Change your targets and reassess your alignment with every swing. If you can get your alignment correct on the practice tee every time, then you are ready to take it to the course and get the same results you produced on the driving range. Consistency in your practice is important. When hitting golf balls on the range, go through the same motions every time with every club. This will give you a routine you repeat, no matter your target.

Just as you would on the course, ensure that you are finishing the swing. When you finish, the club will be over the left shoulder, the shoulders will be level, and the right knee and shoulder will face the target. Hold the finish until the ball hits the ground. This will help you achieve maximum clubhead speed. The club will move through the hitting area the same way every time, creating a repeatable shot pattern and helping you transition successfully to the course.

If you are on the practice tee revisiting the fundamentals and making a modification to your swing, understand that this will take time. Don't get discouraged! Your muscles have gotten accustomed to particular moves and you are now reprogramming them. Once you have successfully made the modification you are looking for, do it over and over and over again. Don't rely on luck or coincidence; you have to ensure that you have retrained your body.

Chapter 22:
Troubleshooting and Frequently Asked Questions

How can I get More Distance?

This is one of the most frequently asked questions in golf. To increase your distance is to increase your clubhead speed. To increase your clubhead speed, you need to make your stance wider, which allows your shoulders to rotate more.

Open your legs to stretch your back left quadrant. This is before making the adjustment:

This is after making the adjustment:

Push back with your left arm and extend your arms back as far as they will go, high and right of your head. Remember the stretched muscle, like a spring, that is loaded and accelerates through the hitting area when released. Don't let your hands drop behind your head at the top of the backswing, as we discussed in Chapter 20, "The Full Swing" or you will throw the club outward on the downswing and lose speed.

Also, practicing with a weighted club will develop the muscles to swing the club faster through impact, which will create more distance.

How do I Correct a Slice?

A slice is one of the most common and recurrent problems in golf; it is the accidental curving of the ball's flight from left to right. 99% of amateur golfers slice the golf ball for one of several reasons:

A- The shoulders are not square. If divots are going to the left of your target line, it may be that your shoulders are aligned in that direction. Turn your shoulders to the right, or into the target, to keep the clubface on line to your intended target.

B- The left hand is in a weak position, i.e., turned to the left. You need to see 2 to 3 knuckles of the left hand when you place your hand on the club. Rotate your hand further to the right until you see those 2 to 3 knuckles.

C- The player does not release the hands through the hitting area, thus not squaring the clubface to the intended target. If the left hand is in a weak position, it is more difficult for the hands to release. By having the left hand in a strong position with the left thumb on the right side of the shaft, you will have the leverage at the top of the swing to pull the club back down with the left hand. Your hands will release from the cocked position to speed up your swing as the club squares through impact.

You can teach your hands to release through the hitting area, practice the exercise we discussed in Chapter 7, under the 10 Full Finger Grip. Place the golf ball on a tee, put your feet together, grip the club shaft with your hands 1 to 1.5 inches apart, and take a full swing. Your separated hands will allow the centrifugal force of the club to square the face at impact, so the ball flight will be straight or right to left, but not a slice. This exercise may take some practice to achieve the correct timing and ball flight.

D- As the player swings the club back, the right leg straightens, as discussed in "The Top of the Backswing" section in Chapter 20, "The

Full Swing." This puts the player in a position in which they cannot pull the club down from the top of the swing. When the right leg is locked, the player then has to throw the club out over the top with their right side. You can avoid this issue by keeping your leg flexible.

<u>If you have tried trouble-shooting these scenarios and still can't fix your slice, here are a couple of additional techniques to try:</u>

A- Make sure that the club is swinging out as far as it can to the right of the target, or, in to out. Swinging from inside the target line to outside the target line will make the ball turn over from right to left.

The club toe will face the sky on both ends of the swing at hip height. Don't bring the clubhead inside the foot line. If you do, it will be behind you and will go off-plane, and you will end up performing all sorts of manipulations.

B- Hit the ball on the inside corner. This technique corrects the ball's flight path without correcting the errors in your body's positioning, but it works.

How do I Avoid a Shank Shot?

A "shank" is hit on the shank of the club, the part that connects the clubhead to the shaft. It happens more frequently with the wedges than with other clubs. Here are the reasons it may happen and the fixes:

A- The number 1 reason for a shank shot is that the head is in front of the ball, not behind it, at address:

Make sure that your head is behind the golf ball at address:

There should be a tilt of the shoulders with the left shoulder being higher than the right.

B-The second most common reason is that the left hand is in a weakened position, or too far to the left. Move the left hand to the right to strengthen the position.

C- The ball is played too far back in the stance at address. Change your stance so that the ball is left of center or forward of where you have been playing it.

D- Both hands are gripping the club too tightly, but primarily the right hand is. Hold the club so that you can feel the weight of the clubhead as you swing, this will ensure that you are not gripping the club too tightly.

E- The club is not being released through the hitting area. In order to regain the feel of the club releasing through the hitting area, you will need to temporarily alter your grip. Use the exercise as discussed in Chapter 7, "Grip Types." Take a 10 Full Finger Grip and separate your hands by about 2 inches. Then take a few swings and get the feel of the hands turning through the hitting area.

After you have felt this, and are comfortable with it, try a few balls. After practice, you will be able to start to move your hands closer back together. Depending on the severity of the issue, you should play with the 10 Full Finger Grip for 3 weeks to a month on the wedges. As you make progress, you can go back to your normal grip but remember to not grip too tightly and to feel the clubhead swing.

Another way to work on releasing through impact is to put your right hand over your left on the club, so no part of the right hand is touching the club:

Take a few swings like this and then gradually increase the length of the swing.

Feel the left hand doing the work and not the right, as we discussed in Chapter 16, "The Full Swing." The left hand needs to be the leader in both short shots and longer swings.

<u>What can I do During the Winter?</u>

The winter months can be a productive time for changing the mechanics of your swing. By hitting into a net, the ball flight becomes less important and you can concentrate solely on the change you are trying to make. Focus on the feel of the swing, just like when you practice with your eyes closed. Since you will not have the benefit of observing the actual flight path, you will need to have an instructor present to evaluate your progress against your goals.

You should also use the winter months to maintain or improve your fitness and flexibility. Much time is wasted in the spring when one has lost this focus in the off-season. A good winter exercise is to practice swinging a weighted golf club. This will strengthen the arms, hands, and wrists. As little as 10 to 20 minutes a day will produce results. If you have time, swing for 10 minutes in the morning and 10 minutes in the evening.

Complimenting this with an exercise program that enhances endurance and athleticism will help increase your clubhead speed when you return to the course in the spring. It will ensure that you aren't running out of steam on the 16th tee and that you can hit the ball out of a tall rough. Better conditioning equals better play.

An exercise program that enhances flexibility will also help you move the clubhead faster through impact because there will be less resistance on the part of your body.

When you start playing in the spring, be patient with yourself and don't expect too much. A spring golfer is like a bear coming out of hibernation, he needs time to get back on track!

<u>We've had a Really Wet Spring. What can I do about it?</u>

If it has been a wet season, you may have noticed that you are hitting a lot of fat shots or hitting behind the ball. This happens because the ground is softer and your feet sink about a quarter to half an inch into the ground. To counter this, grip down on the club a quarter to half an inch, this will help you to not hit behind the ball. You will catch the ball first and have more of a sweeping swing.

What Should I do when I am in High Rough?

When you are in high rough and the ball is down deep in the grass, use a more lofted club, like a 7 or 8 iron. To hit the shot, hold the club up above the grass:

If you were to place the club down in the grass, two things can happen. First, the ball may move and cost you a penalty. Second, as you swing, the high rough may grab your club on the way back, alter your rhythm, and cost you the shot.

Can I Play with Bifocals?

Sorry, in my opinion, you can't play golf while wearing bifocals or trifocals. You will drop your head to see out of the top part of the lens in order to see the ball, which drops your chin onto your chest and will stop your shoulder turn during the backswing. This will give you a shorter backswing and will reduce your power and speed to the swing. I recommend wearing distance glasses only so that you won't drop your chin and won't impede your shoulder turn.

Should I Play Right or Left-Handed?

You may be ambidextrous or you may think you are right or left handed. But if you are right eye dominant you need to play right handed, even if you think you are left handed. This can make a remarkable difference in your game.

To determine which eye is dominant, hold your arm out and point your index finger upwards. Choose an object 10 or 20 feet beyond your finger. If you close your left eye and your finger stays on or close to the target, you are probably right eye dominant. To check, close your right eye and if your finger has moved further from the target then you are definitely right eye dominant.

How can I Avoid Anticipating the Hit?

A lot of people anticipate the club striking the ball and when they do so, they squint or close their eyes. When this happens, they lose sight of the ball. I had a student who was making a great swing right up until the end, at which point I noticed she was closing her eyes at impact.

I will share with you what worked for her. You can point a pencil with the eraser tip towards your face and move the pencil back and forth until you don't blink when the eraser approaches your eye.

When playing, always remember to swing through the shot not at it. Keep your breathing calm and steady. Swing through and finish, making the strike just part of the entire sequence. In this way, you will learn to not anticipate it.

Competing makes me Nervous. How Can I Control my Heart Rate?

Great question! To start, you should anticipate that your competition will make their shot so that when they do, you aren't surprised and don't get ruffled.

Next, compete as much as possible. The more you put yourself in pressure situations, the more your mind and body will learn to calm down and not let emotions get the best of you. Through experience, you will learn to suppress and control your heart rate.

Remember your preflight routine and don't let any negatives creep in. Envision the hook or cut shot that you will use to work the ball away from trouble. By working the ball away from trouble or avoiding the temptation to take shots that are difficult or impossible, you will put yourself in a position of confidence instead of one of nervousness. Engage your Mind's Eye, envision the shot, and then execute.

Finally, remember to breathe and enjoy the moment. Golf is the only game played in a garden. Relax and take in the moment, you will increase your awareness of your surroundings, have a better time, and improve your competitive play.

Afterward
On A Personal Note

Hello, my name is Laura Lewis and I've had the privilege of working very closely with Mahrty for the last couple of years on the book you just finished reading. Hopefully you have already experienced a positive impact in your game and are inspired to keep pursuing the principles we've discussed.

I'd like to tell you a little bit more about Mahrty because there are some things he would never say about himself; he'd find them too self-congratulatory or indulgent, but they should be said. Mahrty's life dream, as you have probably already guessed, is to help as many people as possible improve their game of golf.

A game of golf might seem like a minor pleasure to you or to me, not so important in the grand scale. But if there's one thing that Mahrty is even more interested in than golf, it's the people who play the game and the satisfaction they derive from it. And Mahrty has found a way to make golf meaningful to a special segment of people, our veterans, and that is very important indeed.

Every Saturday during the season, Mahrty works with the Wounded Warriors organization in Fort Belvoir, Virginia. From the day Mahrty and I started collaborating on this project, he made it clear that his time with Wounded Warriors was priority number 1, and our meetings never conflicted with that commitment.

Knowing how strong was Mahrty's passion to publish this book, I was intrigued by the one obligation that captured his heart even more. So I asked him about his Saturdays spent with veterans and why it was so special to him.

Mahrty looked up at me from beneath his reader glasses and then reached in his desk drawer and pulled out 5 coins, which he held out in the palm of his hand. "Do you know what Commander Coins are?" he asked. "No." I shook my head.

"A Commander's Coin," he explained, "is given to you from your commander in recognition of exemplary service. If you go to an Officer's club and you don't have a coin, you buy the drinks."

In my interpretation, a Commander's Coin can be given spontaneously in the course of a day's work, which has special merit. It doesn't need approval, ceremony, or running up a chain of command. I picture young men and women flushing with pride at such recognition from their superiors.

Mahrty has been given 4 such coins by officers and a fifth that was designed this year by the PGA. If the coin is recognition of a job well done, when given to a civilian, well, that must be quite something.

Clearly he doesn't do it for the reward, though, as that was an unexpected surprise. Mahrty enjoys giving back to this community because, as he says, "How do you thank someone who has put their life on the line? You make a difference with someone like that, you've made a good difference."

"Some of these people have lost limbs and many have PTSD. Golf enables them to concentrate on something entirely different. It gives them an avenue to get away from it for a few hours. This is a very important piece of the aftermath of our time in Afghanistan and Iraq that we need to deal with. To see them hit the ball and go in the air, to actually accomplish what they want to, is very gratifying."

"Wounded Warriors," he explains, "is trying to find a way to heal the wounds, mentally and physically. The time on the golf course with instructors gives them something else to concentrate on for a while. They all appreciate the instructors and the program." It goes without saying that Mahrty plans to do this as long as he possibly can and I don't doubt that the last clients he ever works with will be veterans.

The first gentleman who gave Mahrty a coin was a Colonel in the Marines who had his 10-year-old son with him. His son wasn't having a good round at all. Mahrty saw that the boy's left thumb was off the club, so he helped correct the grip. Then the boy started hitting the ball absolutely beautifully and his father was as pleased as he could be.

There was a man in the group who was having difficulty using a wood. Mahrty had him change to a 3 wood from a 5 iron to hit the ball further on a par 5. Then he was able to achieve more distance and by the third shot was on the green.

There was a Marine that had alignment issues. Mahrty squared the man's shoulders; he then hit the ball straighter and was delighted. This is classic Mahrty. He finds the problem and fixes it.

During the round, the Colonel unexpectedly had to leave early but gave Mahrty a Commander's Coin as a parting gift. He said, quite simply, "I can't thank you enough."

A Major in the Air Force gave the second coin to Mahrty. The Major's head rotation wasn't right, which caused manipulations, and cost him the shot. Mahrty helped correct his head rotation at the alignment stage. Then the Major was able to land the ball a foot away from the hole.

Long putts were also an issue for the Major. Mahrty showed him how to go back, imagine the line in his favorite color, walk up, stand over the ball, close his eyes, and stroke the putt. The major closed his eyes and got a putt in at 50 to 60 feet. In Mahrty-speak, he taught the Major how to "turn on the camera upstairs."

There was a gentleman who'd had a stroke and was sitting on the golf cart to take the swing, and "was having a hell of a time." Mahrty showed him how to cock his wrists more and then the player stopped topping the ball. As you will remember, one of Mahrty's key teachings is to learn to play within yourself and the abilities you have. This applies to all of us.

Mahrty's final words on the subject of teaching his students, including veterans, are that you "have to understand the golf swing first in order to adapt the mechanics to the abilities of your students. It's not brain surgery," he says, "you just keep it simple. Most people have a tendency to over-analyze and over-teach. You just need to understand cause and effect. 'Why' is the key. You need to understand why something happens in order to correct it. You should be able to look at the ball flight and understand what happened and apply proper fundamentals to fix the issue."

What does this mean for you, the aspiring golf student? I've thought long and hard on this and because this is Mahrty's book, indeed his life's teachings, I will try to sum this up using his own pearls of wisdom:

Play within yourself and your abilities.

Learn multiple shots so you can take your most strategic shot.

Change your target frequently and don't perfect bad habits.

Pick a target you cannot reach, so you don't decelerate.

Finish your swing or you will alter its path.

A putt that falls short of the hole has no chance of going in. Aim past the hole.

When putting, let the green move the ball for you.

When chipping, let the loft of the club do the work for you, get the ball over the fringe instead of through it.

Be a swinger of the club, not a hitter of the ball.

Develop a positive attitude that cannot be taken away with one swing of the club.

Don't worry about the past or the future. Concentrate on what is right in front of you.

Envision the shot but don't envision a shot you cannot hit.

Develop and engage your senses.

Prepare. Don't neglect your pre-shot routine.

Be courteous of your fellow players.

Always leave the course better than you found it.

And.......Give back.

CPSIA information can be obtained
at www.ICGtesting.com
Printed in the USA
BVOW06s0028180517
483950BV00007B/9/P

9 781634 912518